Making Disciples
Workbook

How To Help People Follow Christ

by David Rhoades

Table of Contents

Preface

This workbook is written for every believer who desires to be obedient to God's call on our lives to become disciple-makers. Pastors such as myself should lead the way, for we are charged with more than simply keeping the aquarium—we should be fishing for men. That is, we should "do the work of an evangelist" (2 Tim. 4:5)[1].

Pastors are "to equip the saints for the work of ministry" (Eph. 4:11-12). Not only should pastors personally fish for men, but they should be helping other believers do the same. This guide was written with that goal in mind.

Disciple-making is for every Christian, not only church leaders. The Lord has allowed us to live in a world with billions of people, and the only effective way to reach them with the gospel is for God's people to be trained to fulfill the Great Commission. Specialized ministries by extraordinary Christians will never even make a significant dent in the number of people without Christ. Regular believers must be encouraged and trained to accomplish this most important work.

Making Disciples Workbook: Personally Leading People to Christ is designed to help you make disciples of the lost people in your life. Although this workbook is designed for self-study, a small group of believers can do the study together. If you are the leader of a small group, just make sure each member of your group has a copy of this workbook. Then as a group, share your answers and discuss the disciple-making principles and insights the Lord has given you.

After completing this workbook, an additional resource called *Spiritual Basics* can help you assist new believers to grow in their faith. Both workbooks may be downloaded for free at davidrhoades.org or purchased on Amazon.com.

Gratitude and Permissions

Some of the stylistic formatting of this workbook comes directly from and with the permission of T4TOnline.org. Much thanks go to Ying Kai, Steve Smith, and David Garrison for their excellent work in assisting people to become better disciple-makers. Other key influences found in this material include the work of Steve Sjogren, Lee Thomas, Randy Raysbrook, and Jim Petersen.

---

[1] Unless otherwise noted, Scripture quotations are from The Holy Bible, English Standard Version® (ESV®), copyright © 2001 by Crossway, a publishing ministry of Good News Publishers. Used by permission. All rights reserved.

Because it is my desire that God use this workbook for the greatest benefit to his Kingdom:

- You may distribute this workbook to others on the condition that you give it to them for free. "Freely you have received, freely give."

- You may translate this workbook into other languages.

- You may make changes to this workbook so that it better fits your setting.

Getting Started

You are capable of leading your lost friends and loved ones to Christ and then helping them grow spiritually. You are uniquely gifted to do this most important work. No written instruction guide, no book, and no website can do what you can do: Be a living witness for Christ before your friends. No one knows your friends like you do, and no one is more concerned than you for their eternal salvation and spiritual health.

Remember: You are not in this alone. God has prepared his entire family to assist you. So as you pray for your lost friends, ask other Spirit-filled believers to pray with you. If (and when!) your friends come to Christ, remember that they will need a spiritual family. You may be very instrumental not only in assisting your friends to grow, but also in introducing them to a larger spiritual family—people who can provide an exponentially greater amount of encouragement and instruction than you can provide alone.

A special note: Some people who come to faith in Christ may not easily "fit" into the culture of some churches. These new believers still need a spiritual family. The "church" some new believers need may have some untraditional forms—forms that may be surprisingly more like the 1st-century church than what many of us experience. Whatever happens, avoid the temptation to "give up" on your lost loved ones just because you think they wouldn't fit into your church.

My prayer is that God uses you to accomplish his task of making disciples of your loved ones. The Lord Jesus, who has been given all authority in heaven and earth, has promised to be with you each step of the way (Matthew 28:18-20)!

In Christ,

Dr. David H. Rhoades

Session 1

Disciple-Making — Our One Purpose

overview

God's plan has always been to have a kingdom inhabited with people who believe in him. This was true before sin entered the world, and it remains true today.

When God created humans, he gave us the freedom to obey or disobey him. When Adam and Eve disobeyed God, he did not give up on his plan to have a kingdom of believers. God intervened, providing mercy and grace to those who would believe in him. His promise ultimately was fulfilled in the person and work of Jesus Christ, the Son of God. And "to all who did receive him, to those who believed in his name, he gave the right to become children of God" (John 1:12).

In God's wisdom, he has given us—his children—the privilege and responsibility of sharing this good news with those who do not yet believe in Christ. We are left on earth and not transferred directly to heaven the moment we trust Christ so we can help others follow Jesus—to be disciple-makers. In this session, you will discover what biblical disciple-making is.

digging deeper

The Great Commission

In your Bible, read the following passage and fill in the blanks:[2]

> And Jesus came and said to them, "All authority in heaven and on earth has been given to me. _____ therefore and _____ _____ of all nations, _____ them in the name of the Father and of the Son and of the Holy Spirit, _____ them to observe all that I have commanded you. And behold, I am with you always, to the end of the age."
>
> *Matthew 28:18-20*

---

[2] Suggested answers are located in the last section of this workbook.

Of the four verbs in these verses, *"go...baptize...teach"* are supporting verbs that show us how to carry out the one imperative command: *"make disciples."* We do this by going to the nations with the gospel, baptizing those that believe, and teaching them to follow Jesus.

looking closer

Disciple-Making is the Task of All Believers

Jesus did not limit the Great Commission to church leaders. It is for all of us. Pastors are called to equip all of God's people to become disciple-makers.

Jesus designed you to be a disciple-maker. He saved you for this purpose. You bring an understanding, perspectives, and experiences that not only are uniquely yours, but that your friends and loved ones need to hear.

- Do you know people who need the Lord? (Circle YES or NO)   YES   NO
  Even if the answer is "NO," keep going with this workbook!
  You will soon learn some principles on how to befriend people
  who don't know Christ.

- Do you know how to lead your friends to Christ?   YES   NO

- Do you know how to help your friends grow in their faith after   YES   NO
  they believe?

Disciple-Making is a Process that Begins with Evangelism

A close examination of the Great Commission reveals just how comprehensive the task of making disciples is. According to Jesus, disciple-making begins as we go to "the nations" (literally, "the peoples") with the message of the gospel. The gospel is the story of Jesus.

Read 1 Peter 3:18. How does this verse connect the story of Jesus to our lives today?

_____

_____

_____

Disciple-Making is a Process that Continues with Spiritual Growth

Discipleship is more than spiritual growth after salvation. It is a comprehensive process that includes both evangelism and spiritual growth. If evangelism alone is the goal, then we would simply make converts, not disciples.

Why do you think it is important to help new believers grow?

_____

_____

Disciple-Making is a Process that Results in More Disciple-Making

Jesus' plan is for his followers to produce more followers. Disciple-making has not been fulfilled until the disciple has become a disciple-maker himself.

Why is it important for the people you disciple to become disciple-makers? _____

_____

_____

Disciple-Making Defined

A close look at the Great Commission helps give us a simple, comprehensive definition of disciple-making:

> **Disciple-making is the process of bringing people from unbelief to becoming devoted followers of Jesus who reproduce this process with others.**

reflect

1. Who was most instrumental in leading you to Christ? _____

2. Did he or she personally (1-on-1) continue to help you follow Jesus? _____

3. On a scale of 1 to 10 (1 being poor and 10 being great), how would you rate yourself as a disciple-maker? _____

4. Which of the following do you need to learn and put into practice? (Circle all that apply)

   Befriending lost people

   Praying for my lost loved ones, friends, and acquaintances

   Sharing God's Word with inquisitive people

   Leading someone to Christ

   Helping a new believer grow spiritually

Session 2

Farming & Parenting — How God's Kingdom Grows

overview

As we have seen, disciple-making consists of two connected components: **evangelism and spiritual growth.**

The goal of evangelism is to bring lost people to faith in Christ. The Holy Spirit—not you—produces conversion. Yet he has given you the incredible opportunity and responsibility of having a role in the evangelism process. God saves lost people as we (1) befriend and pray for them, (2) share God's Word with them, and (3) tell the gospel to them.

The goal of spiritual growth is to help believers become more like Christ. Just like with evangelism, the Holy Spirit—not you—produces spiritual growth as believers yield themselves to God. Yet he has given us a role in the spiritual growth of others. God grows believers as we provide them with (1) loving care, (2) a personal example to follow and (3) biblical instruction.

In this session, you will discover how you can be involved in God's work of helping a person follow Jesus and begin to grow spiritually.

digging deeper

There are many ways to participate in evangelism, and there are many ways to help someone grow spiritually. But does the Bible give us a simple, yet comprehensive, disciple-making plan? Yes.

In the Bible, the most widely used analogy to picture **evangelism** is **farming**. And the most widely used analogy to picture **spiritual growth** is **parenting**. These two ideas establish the basis of a biblical disciple-making strategy.

Evangelism = Plowing + Planting + Harvesting

Read the following passages of Scripture and write down words or phrases associated with **farming:**

Mark 4:26-29 - _____

Mark 4:31-32 - _____

Psalm 126:5-6 - _____

John 4:35 - _____

Matthew 9:36-38 - _____

Before a farmer can harvest his crops, he must plant seeds. And unless he is planting seed in "good soil," he must be ready to plow the field. The same principles are true in evangelism.

As disciple-makers, **we are farmers working with the lost.** God's Word instructs us how we can assist the lost people in our lives to follow Christ, regardless of how hard the soil of their hearts might be. If a person's heart is hard, we can befriend him and pray for him. If a person's heart is receptive, we can plant the seed of God's Word in his life. And if a person is ready to be saved, we can share the gospel with him.

> **Plowing** = Befriending and praying for those far from Christ
>
> **Planting** = Sharing God's Word with inquiring seekers
>
> **Harvesting** = Leading a willing receiver to Christ

Spiritual Growth = Nurturing + Modeling + Teaching

Read the following passages of Scripture and write down the words or phrases associated with parenting:

Galatians 4:19 - _____

1 Thessalonians 2:7 - _____

1 Peter 2:2 - _____

1 John 2:1 - _____

Hebrews 5:13 - _____

Every parent must provide his or her child with loving care, a personal example, and instructions on how to live. Likewise, new believers need a spiritual parent to provide them with these necessities. And who is a better spiritual parent than someone who was instrumental in leading them to faith in Christ?

As disciple-makers, we are parents. God's Word instructs us how we can assist new believers to grow in Christ. When a person comes to faith in Christ, we must affirm and love him. The new believer also needs a living example of how a Christian lives, as well as our help as he begins to seek nourishment from God's Word.

> **Nurturing** = Affirming and loving new believers
>
> **Modeling** = Being a living example of a Spirit-filled Christian
>
> **Teaching** = Providing the nourishment of God's Word

Review the definition of disciple-making: **Disciple-making is the process of bringing people from unbelief to becoming devoted followers of Jesus who reproduce this process with others.**

disciple-making ladder

The process of making a disciple of Jesus can be illustrated with a "Disciple-Making Ladder." We must do our part as God draws our friends and loved ones up the ladder.

If My Friend Is...	I Can Provide...
A New Baptized Believer Has received Jesus & been baptized	**Parenting** A loving, modeling, and teaching relationship
A Willing Receiver Is ready to receive Jesus	**Harvesting** The gospel and baptism after salvation
An Inquiring Seeker Has questions about spirituality/God	**Planting** God's Word in spoken and written form
A Disinterested Unbeliever Is lost with little or no interest in Jesus	**Plowing** Friendship & intercessory prayer
If My Friend Is...	**I Can Provide...**

In the following sessions, we'll take a closer look at the steps of biblical disciple-making. Most importantly, you will discover some simple, effective ways to engage in the processes of plowing, planting, harvesting, and parenting.

reflect

1. Who is a lost person you know? If you don't know the person's name, how might you describe him or her (such as "waiter" or "sales clerk")?

   _____

2. As far as you know, which description in the Disciple-Making Ladder best describes your friend (such as "Disinterested Unbeliever")?

   _____

3. Are you willing to do your part as a disciple-maker and leave the results to God?

   _____

Session 3

Plowing (Part 1) – Cultivating Friendships

overview

Jesus said, "Love your _____ as yourself" (*Matthew 22:39*).

For many Christians, the thought of getting to know lost people—much less *love* them—is frightening. Studies show that it only takes a few months for a new believer to lose the vast majority of his friendships with those who do not yet know Christ. As he leaves behind some of his old habits, his friends leave him. By the time the new believer has learned how to share his faith, he may come to the conclusion that he doesn't have much of an audience. So how can a Christian lead others to Christ when all of his friends are saved?

Whether you've been following Christ for a long time or you are a new believer, God uses your words and actions to draw people to himself. This occurs through the power of relationships.

In this session, you will discover how to make friends with people who have little or no interest in Jesus Christ. It is friendship with a vision—a friendship that loves people so deeply that we envision what it might look like if they began following Jesus.

digging deeper

Read Luke 8:4-15.

The seed (God's Word) remained the same in all four instances, but the results were different. Why did the seed in verse 8 yield a great harvest? It fell into _____ _____.

The lost people in our lives are like the soil Jesus described. Some are "good soil," ready to receive God's Word. Others are "hard ground," showing little or no interest in following Jesus. They may be like Paul's description of false teachers in Ephesians 4:18 – *They are darkened in their understanding, alienated from the life of God because of the ignorance that is in them, due to their hardness of heart.*

What does God want?

God *"desires _____ _____ to be saved and to come to the knowledge of the truth"* (1 Timothy 2:4). "All" includes those whose hearts are hard toward him. Your friendship with a lost person may be very instrumental in helping that person follow Christ.

What should I avoid?

You cannot force or manipulate anyone into believing in Christ. The authors of the book *Irresistible Evangelism* describe "seven deadly sins of evangelism"[3]:

- *Scheming* – Tricking someone into hearing the gospel
- *Scalp hunting* – Treating someone as if he is just a number or a means to grow your church
- *Screaming* – Being rude because you are convinced you are right
- *Selling* – Convincing people to say yes to Jesus as if he were some kind of commodity
- *Stalking* – Never giving people a chance to make a thoughtful decision
- *Sermonizing* – Being a Christian who has all the answers
- *Spectating* – Being too afraid to help people follow Jesus

🔭 looking closer

So what are the elements necessary to become friends with people who do not yet know Christ?

Element #1: Noticing

Have you ever heard a Christian say, "I don't know any lost people"? The reality is that there are lost people all around us, but sometimes we fail to notice them. Once you start noticing people, you start caring about them.

> **Noticing Assignment:** The next time you spend 30 minutes or more in the community (out of the house and away from your church campus), write down a description or name of the people you encounter: the barista, the person you work with, etc. Notice how many lost people are in your peripheral vision.

---

[3] For additional tips relating to servant evangelism, see *Irresistible Evangelism*, by Steve Sjogren, Dave Ping, and Doug Pollock (www.kindnessresources.com).

Element #2: Small Acts of Kindness

Wherever you go, preach the gospel. And if you must, use words. - Francis of Assisi

Jesus used acts of kindness to demonstrate his love. The Bible says that Jesus *"went about _____ _____ and healing all who were oppressed by the devil, for God was with him"* (Acts 10:38).

Serving lost people with small acts of kindness tears down walls and opens hearts. When you do something kind for a lost person, expect nothing in return—even if the person finds it difficult to receive. You are helping him or her learn how to receive God's grace.

A heart that loves finds a thousand ways.
A heart that doesn't finds a thousand excuses. - Middle Eastern Proverb

---

Kindness Assignment: Find one item that you have at your disposal right now (a pen, your shoes, a bottle of water, etc.), and think of one way you can use that item to serve someone in Christ's name during the coming week.

What is your idea? _____

_____

_____

_____

Element #3: Learning to Listen

"Treat people the same way you want them to treat you" (Matthew 7:12, NASB).

If you want people to listen to you, learn to listen to them first. You must respect people's beliefs—even if you believe they are wrong—if you want them to respect yours. People have the right to listen to you or shut you out. Listening is the only way to earn the right to be heard.

Talking has the goal of being correct, but listening has the goal of understanding what someone else is saying.

By asking questions of others, you can begin to understand them. You show them that you can feel what they are feeling—that you care. Through listening, compassion grows in your heart.

Listening Assignment: This week, ask a lost person about himself or herself without discussing yourself at all. If it is a person you do not know, you may have to pay special attention to something he says or does. For example, if he mentions his children, you can ask questions about them.

Who might you seek out to listen to this week? _____

---

reflect

1. **Noticing Assignment:** Write the names or descriptions of some lost people in your life:

   _____

   _____

   _____

2. **Kindness Assignment:** What were the results of your idea? _____

   _____

   _____

   _____

3. **Listening Assignment:** What did you learn about the person you listened to?

   _____

   _____

   _____

Session 4

Plowing (Part 2) – Preparing Hearts Through Prayer

🔭 overview

God has chosen us to have a vital role in disciple-making. Not only are we the ones who take the message of the gospel to the lost, but <u>our prayers move God to save</u>.

> *"Around us is a world lost in sin,*
> *above us is a God willing and able to save it;*
> *it is ours to build the bridge that links heaven and earth,*
> *and prayer is the mighty instrument that does the work."* - E.M. Bounds

God expects us to pray for the lost. During Isaiah's ministry, the nation of Israel was in a terrible situation. Just like the condition of lost people in your life, no one but God could deliver them. The Lord observed that, in spite of their hopelessness, no one was praying: *"He saw that there was no man—He was amazed that there was no one interceding"* (Isaiah 59:16, HCSB). If we do not pray for the lost to be saved, who will?

According to the New Testament, every Christian is a priest. This means, in part, that we represent lost people to the Father, interceding on their behalf. God the Father moves when his people pray for that which he already desires. Jesus said, *"If you abide in me, and my words abide in you, ask _____ you wish, and it will be done for you. By this my Father is glorified, that you _____ _____ _____ and so prove to be my disciples"* (John 15:7-8).

In this session, you will discover how to pray for the lost people in your life.

🛠 digging deeper

The Condition of the Lost

The Bible uses vivid images to describe people without Christ. Read each correlating Scripture to discover the impact of God's view of the lost. People without Christ are:

- _____ by the devil – 2 Timothy 2:26
- _____ in a strong man's house – Luke 11:14-23 (Hint: Satan is the strong man, but Jesus is the Stronger Man)

- Under the _____ of the evil one – 1 John 5:19
- _____ of the devil – John 8:43-44
- _____ in sin – Ephesians 2:1
- _____ by Satan – Ephesians 2:2 (Hint: The word "work" means "to be energized or empowered")
- _____ to the gospel – 2 Corinthians 4:3-4

With our lost loved ones in such a terrible condition, it is imperative that we understand that we are in a battle for souls. The only way they will ever follow Jesus is if God does a work in their lives, and he moves when we pray.

The Scheme of the Enemy: Deception

Satan will not give up lost people without a fight. The devil and his forces seek to interrupt your prayers for the lost, but the Holy Spirit in you is greater than Satan (see 1 John 4:4).

Sometimes our prayers become weakened because of sin or unbelief in our hearts. Paul instructs us, *"Put on the whole armor of God, that you may be able to stand against the schemes of the devil"* (Ephesians 6:11).

As you pray to your Heavenly Father, who is greater than all, remember to depend on the Lord for victory. Hebrews 2:14 says, *"Through death [Jesus] might destroy the one who has the power of death, that is, the devil."*

How does Satan hold people in spiritual captivity? Through **deception**. Satan cannot do anything on his own authority except lie. *"When he lies, he speaks out of his own character, for he is a _____ and the _____ ___ _____"* (John 8:44).

When Satan lies to unbelievers, it is designed to keep them from believing in Jesus. When he lies to believers, it is designed to keep us weak and ineffective. The pattern of Satan's lies to believers is always the same:

Satan's Lies
↓
Unbelief and Sin
↓
Discouragement
↓
Weak or No Prayer

The Power of God's Word

"Sanctify them in the truth; your word is truth" (*John 17:17*).

The only effective weapon against Satan's lies is the truth of God's Word. In each instance that Jesus encountered Satan's lies, Jesus quoted Scripture (see Matthew 4:1-11). Jesus hid God's Word in his heart, and we must do the same.

We will discover more about this principle in Session 5.

Attitudes of Prayer

Remain humble. Confess your sins. Keep on the armor of God (cf. Ephesians 6:11-18).

Intercede with the right motive: God's glory (cf. John 15:8). Praying for a good thing with the wrong motive (such as a parent praying for a child to be saved out of pride for the family name) will render your prayers null and void.

Pray with faith. The Great Commission—our command to be disciple-makers—begins with Jesus saying, "All authority in heaven and on earth has been given to me" (Matthew 28:18). We must believe that Jesus can save the lost, and we must pray like it. Jesus gave us the authority to attack the gates of hell (cf. Matthew 16:18-19).

🔭 looking closer

How to Pray for the Lost[4]

Pray for lost people by name.

- Pray for God to bless the person. *"God's kindness is meant to lead you to _____"* (Romans 2:4).

- Pray for the Holy Spirit to convict the person without Christ. Jesus said the Holy Spirit *"will convict the world concerning sin and righteousness and judgment: concerning sin, because they do not _____ in me"* (John 16:8-9).

- Pray for God to illuminate the lost person's mind. *"For God...has shone in our hearts to give the light of the knowledge of the glory of God in the face of Jesus Christ"* (2 Corinthians 4:6).

---

[4] For additional tips in praying for the lost, see *Praying Effectively for the Lost* by Lee Thomas (www.pelministries.org).

Pray for the person who shares the gospel. God may allow you to be the witness, or he may have someone else share the gospel with the person. Whomever the witness is, pray that the gospel will be presented clearly and boldly. *"[Pray] that I may make it _____, which is how I ought to speak"* (Colossians 4:4).

Pray for an open door to share the gospel. Paul asked the church at Colossae to pray for him as he shared the gospel: *"Continue steadfastly in prayer, being watchful in it with thanksgiving. At the same time, pray also for us, that God may open to us a door for the word, to declare the mystery of Christ"* (Colossians 4:2-3).

reflect

1. What specific strategies does Satan use to cause discouragement and a lack of effective prayer in your life?

    _____

    _____

    _____

    _____

2. Who is someone (or multiple people) that you will pray for today and on a regular basis?

    _____

    _____

    _____

    _____

Session 5

Planting — Spreading God's Word

🔭 overview

As you **befriend** (Session 3) and **pray for** (Session 4) lost people in your life, God will begin to turn their hearts into "good soil." It may take longer than you wish, so be patient. Keep plowing the ground with love and prayer.

> And let us not grow weary of doing good, for in due season we will reap, if we ____ _____ _____ ____ (*Galatians 6:9*).

When a person without Christ is receptive to the things of God, your task is simple: plant seeds. In other words, tell the person what God's Word says. But how do you know when a person is receptive, and what kind of "seed" should you plant?

In this session, you will discover how to tell when someone in your life is interested in Christ, as well as what to do at that point.

🔨 digging deeper

How To Know When Someone Is Receptive to God

We are not mind-readers. There is only one way we can know what God is doing in someone's heart: <u>Listen to their words</u>. A person's words expose his or her heart.

> "For the mouth speaks out of that which _____ the heart." (*Matthew 12:34*).

When lost people in your life start to ask questions about Jesus or the Bible or about spiritual things, take notice. It means their hearts may be softening. The Lord is making effective your prayers and love.

Many times people are receptive to God when facing a crisis or other stresses (such as a move or a new baby). Sometimes people are receptive when religious ideas are part of a larger social discussion (such as at Easter). But people are almost always most receptive toward someone they know rather than strangers.

In **Luke 10:1-11**, Jesus directed his disciples to share the gospel with a "son of peace" (a receptive man) who had influence over his household. The people in man's sphere of influence would in turn be receptive to him. The disciples later continued this methodology to spread the gospel rapidly in the first century (see the use of the word "house" or "household" in Acts 5:42; 11:13-14; 16:15, 30-34).

<u>People without Christ are most receptive to people they know—people in their sphere of influence.</u>

What To Do When Someone Is Receptive to God

When someone is receptive to God, we simply plant the seed of God's Word in his heart. In other words, speak God's Word to inquiring seekers. With gentleness, tell them what the Bible says about their question.

In 2 Timothy 2:24, we learn that the Lord's servant must correct his opponents *"with _____. God may perhaps grant them repentance leading to a knowledge of the truth."*

In the course of normal conversations, you can begin to plant the seed of God's Word in the good soil of lost people you know. When a complete gospel presentation is not possible, you can still show how the Bible is relevant to their lives.

But What Should I Say?

There are numerous resources and books that can give you or inquiring seekers biblical guidance.[5] But there is no substitute for speaking God's Word to someone else in the course of normal conversation. To do this, you first must have God's Word in *your* mind and heart. You can only plant the seeds that you possess.

Psalm 119:11-16 gives us advice on how to possess the Word of God within us.

<u>Treasure God's Word in your heart</u>. *"I have stored up your word in my _____, that I might not sin against you"* (Psalm 119:11). To memorize a verse of Scripture, follow these steps:

- Read a verse in your Bible.
- Say it out loud.
- Say it out loud without looking.

---

[5] One of the best topical Scripture guides on the Internet is found at www.openbible.info/topics.

Ask God to teach you his Word. *"Blessed are you, O Lord; teach me your statutes!"* (Psalm 119:12). The Holy Spirit must your Teacher.

Teach God's Word to others. *"With my lips I declare all the rules of your mouth"* (Psalm 119:13). The best students are teachers.

Rejoice in God's Word. *"In the way of your testimonies I delight as much as in all riches... I will delight in your statutes; I will not forget your word"* (Psalm 119:14, 16).

Meditate on God's Word. *"I will meditate on your precepts and fix my eyes on your ways"* (Psalm 119:15).

reflect

Whatever date today is, read that corresponding chapter in the **Book of Proverbs**. For example, if today is the 12th day of the month, read Proverbs 12. With 31 chapters, reading one chapter each day will enable you to start possessing the seeds of God's wisdom to plant in the heart of others.

In your reading, what truths did the Holy Spirit bring to your attention?

_____

_____

_____

_____

_____

_____

_____

_____

_____

_____

Session 6

Harvesting — Introducing People to Christ

👓 overview

**Those who sow in tears shall _____ with shouts of joy!
He who goes out weeping, bearing the seed for sowing, shall come home
with shouts of joy, bringing his sheaves with him (*Psalm 126:5-6*)**

The harvest is a joy for the farmer. Likewise, there is nothing more exciting than helping someone receive Christ.

Using the analogy of giving birth, Jesus described receiving him this way: *"Truly, truly, I say to you, unless one is _____ _____ he cannot see the kingdom of God"* (John 3:3). The new birth is an act of the Holy Spirit, and he is looking for people who will care for his children.

In this session, you will discover **when** and **how** to share Jesus with someone. And remember this: **every time you introduce someone to Jesus, you cannot fail**. It is God's work—not yours—to turn a person's heart to him. Jesus said, *"No one can come to Me unless the Father who sent Me draws him"* (John 6:44). If you share Jesus with someone and they do not receive him, you did not fail! You were faithful with the Good News!

🛠 digging deeper

When to Share Jesus

The Holy Spirit dwells in your life, and he will prompt you and guide you as you help your friends follow Jesus. Learn to listen to him. Ask the Holy Spirit when you should speak.

You also need to listen to your lost friend. While it is never a bad idea to share the gospel, your friend will usually tell you that he is ready. He may say something like:

- "I've been thinking about Jesus. Tell me more."

- "How do you think a person gets to heaven?"

- "I want what you have."

reflect

How To Share Jesus

Part 1: Write out your story with three parts:

Your life before Jesus: _____

_____

_____

_____

_____

_____

How you met Jesus: _____

_____

_____

_____

_____

_____

Your life since meeting Jesus: _____

_____

_____

_____

_____

_____

Part 2: Practice sharing the good news of Jesus by drawing out this bridge illustration featuring Romans 6:23:[6]

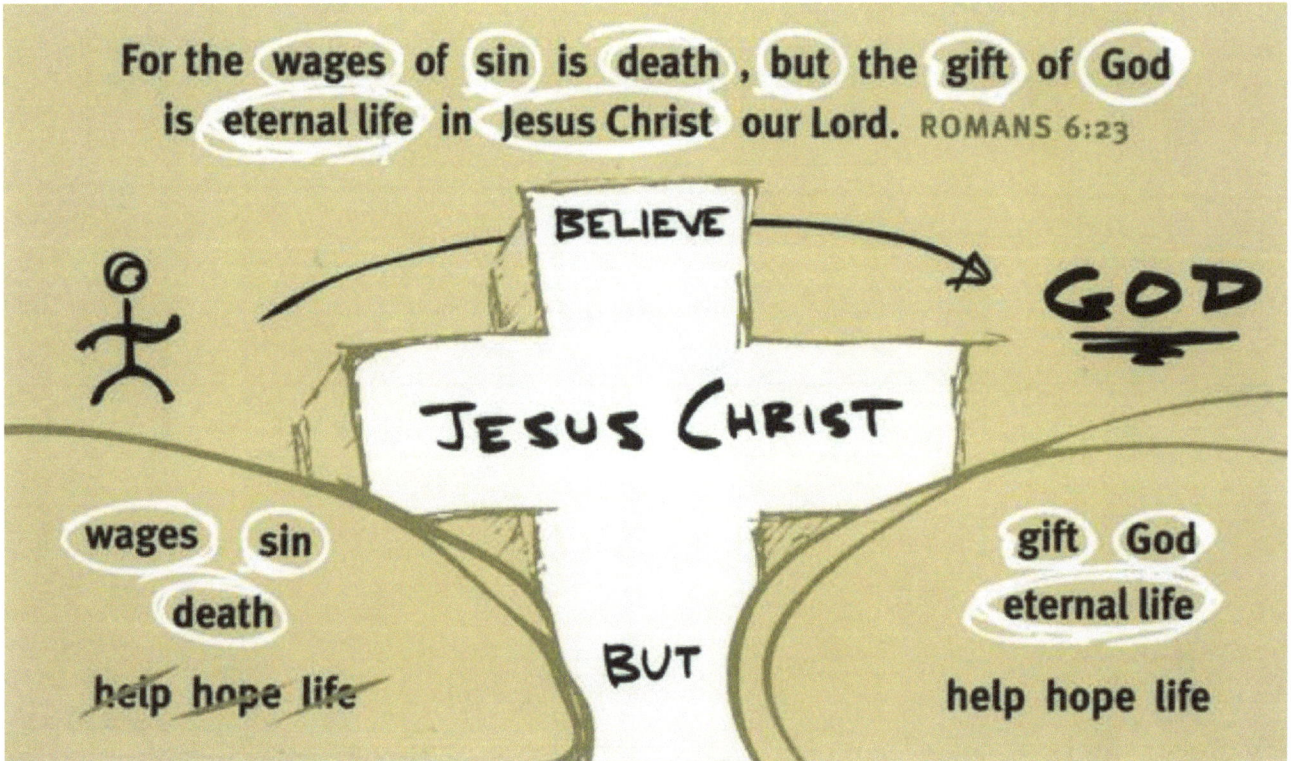

[6] Used by permission from NavPress, all rights reserved. ONE VERSE EVANGELISM, © 2000 by Randy Raysbook. http://www.navpress.com/product/9780972902366/One-Verse-Evangelism-Randy-Raysbrook-and-Steve-Walker.

Session 7

Parenting — Helping a New Believer Grow

overview

As we discovered in Session 2, the most prevalent analogy in the Bible that describes bringing a lost person to faith in Christ is farming. But once a person receives Christ, their new journey is best described by the analogy of parenting.

When a baby is born, none of us would say to it, "Well, I'm glad you're here. Let me give you a few instructions: You'll want to feed and water yourself. And make sure you clean yourself. Our family lives just a few miles away. Hope to see you there soon." A baby needs more nurture and care than that.

New believers need an extra level of care and attention. They are God's children, and he expects us to care for them. In this session, you will discover the importance of baptism and one-on-one spiritual parenting.

digging deeper

Baptism

When we think about baptism[7], there are <u>five questions</u> to answer:

1. **Why?** Jesus commanded it (Matthew 28:19-20). It is symbolic of death to sin and being made alive to righteousness (Romans 6:1-6)

2. **Where?** In water (Mark 1:9-11)

3. **Who?** A follower of Jesus (John 4:1-2; Matthew 28:19-2; 1 Corinthians 1:10-17; Acts 10:47-48)

4. **How?** Immersion (Mark 1:9-11)

5. **When?** Immediately (Acts 8:36-38)

When a nail is cinched, it is driven through wood and then bent down on the other side,

---

7   For a brief, yet comprehensive study on baptism, visit <u>www.t4tonline.org/wp-content/uploads/2011/02/3b-Baptism-resources.pdf</u>.

securing it from being pulled out. Baptism is similar to that, in that it connects a very memorable experience to the new believer's relationship with Christ. Baptism should be the first act of obedience of a new believer.

Baptism has also been described to be like a wedding ring. It is an outward, public display of a commitment of the heart. Encourage the person you lead to Christ to be baptized as soon as possible.

One-on-One Spiritual Parenting

As we have seen in Session 2, one-on-one spiritual parenting is biblical. It provides:

> **Nurturing** = Affirming and loving new believers
>
> **Modeling** = Being a living example of a Spirit-filled Christian
>
> **Teaching** = Providing the nourishment of God's Word

Many Christians feel unequipped to be a spiritual parent simply because they never had it modeled to them. Instead, many of us have grown accustomed to a two-level approach to spiritual growth of (1) large-scale worship and (2) small groups.

However, a new Christian may have very intense or intimate questions that must be addressed if he is to grow as he should. Both large-scale worship and small groups are good, but neither approach can give a deep level of <u>intimate, personalized life-transformation</u>. *That* requires one-on-one interaction in an atmosphere of mutual trust, transparency, and confidentiality—a spiritual parent.

> *But we were _____ among you, like a nursing _____ taking care of her own children* (1 Thessalonians 2:7).

Sometimes a spiritual parent will be **like a mother** of a newborn. The most important thing a mother can give her infant is not information, nor is it to correct every mistake the child makes. A mother gives individualized attention and care to each child, making them secure in her love and acceptance.

> *For you know how, like a _____ with his children, we _____ each one of you and _____ you and charged you to walk in a manner worthy of God, who calls you into his own kingdom and glory* (1 Thessalonians 2:11-12).

Sometimes a spiritual parent will be **like a father**. A father instills confidence in his child with exhortation and encouragement. When a child says, "I can't," a father replies, "I'm with you. We'll do it together." New believers need someone like that to cheer for them.

The people you lead to Christ need a spiritual parent here on earth that they can follow.

Remember the Goal: Reproducing Disciples

Maturity is the desired end. In the physical world, maturity occurs when a plant, tree, or animal reproduces. The spiritual disciples you make will reproduce, continuing the chain of spiritual generations. This is the key to fulfilling the Great Commission.

> "The primary objective in discipleship is to bring your disciple to the point of 'digging his own well' (to drink from the Word) and lose his dependence on you."
> -Chris Adist in *Personal Disciple Making*

reflect

Practically speaking, if you lead someone to Christ, <u>what do you do next</u>?

- Encourage your friend to be **baptized**.

- Get your friend a **Bible** if he does not have one already.

- Keep your friend in close **fellowship** with other Christians—including yourself. His new spiritual family can provide him with friendship and guidance.

- Help your friend **grow** spiritually. One resource that may help is another workbook called *Spiritual Basics*. It has a handful of spiritual nourishment lessons that you can download for free at davidrhoades.org or purchase at Amazon.com. When you lead someone to Christ, offer to meet together (perhaps once a week). You can give your friend a copy of *Spiritual Basics* and suggest working through it together.

Appendix – Suggested Answers

Session 1

Matthew 28:18-20 – *And Jesus came and said to them, "All authority in heaven and on earth has been given to me. <u>Go</u> therefore and <u>make</u> <u>disciples</u> of all nations, <u>baptizing</u> them in the name of the Father and of the Son and of the Holy Spirit, <u>teaching</u> them to observe all that I have commanded you. And behold, I am with you always, to the end of the age."*

1 Peter 3:18 tells us why Jesus died: to bring us to God. People today need to hear that message.

It is important to help new believers grow so they will become strong in their faith and continue to follow Jesus every day.

The people I disciple must become disciple-makers because there are lost people in their lives that they are uniquely suited to reach for Christ.

Session 2

Mark 4:26-29 – seed, ground, sprouts, grows, blade, ear, grain, ripe, sickle, harvest
Mark 4:31-32 – grain, seed, sown, grows
Psalm 126:5-6 – sow, reap, seed, sheaves
John 4:35 – harvest, fields, white for harvest
Matthew 9:36-38 – harvest, laborers, Lord of the harvest, his harvest

Galatians 4:19 – little children, childbirth
1 Thessalonians 2:7 – nursing mother taking care of her own children
1 Peter 2:2 – newborn infants, pure spiritual milk, grow up
1 John 2:1 – little children
Hebrews 5:13 – milk, child

Session 3

"Love your <u>neighbor</u> as yourself" (Matthew 22:39).

It fell into <u>good</u> <u>soil</u>.

God *"desires <u>all</u> <u>people</u> (or <u>all</u> <u>men</u>) to be saved and to come to the knowledge of the truth"* (1 Timothy 2:4).

The Bible says that Jesus *"went about <u>doing</u> <u>good</u> and healing all who were oppressed by the devil, for God was with him"* (Acts 10:38).

Session 4

Jesus said, *"If you abide in me, and my words abide in you, ask <u>whatever</u> you wish, and it will be done for you. By this my Father is glorified, that you <u>bear</u> <u>much</u> <u>fruit</u> and so prove to be my disciples"* (John 15:7-8).

- <u>Captured</u> by the devil – 2 Timothy 2:26
- <u>Possessions</u> in a strong man's house – Luke 11:14-23 (Hint: Satan is the strong man, but Jesus is the Stronger Man)
- Under the <u>sway</u> of the evil one – 1 John 5:19
- <u>Children</u> of the devil – John 8:43-44
- <u>Dead</u> in sin – Ephesians 2:1
- <u>Empowered</u> by Satan – Ephesians 2:2 (Hint: The word "work" means "to be energized or empowered")
- <u>Blinded</u> to the gospel – 2 Corinthians 4:3-4

"When he lies, he speaks out of his own character, for he is a <u>liar</u> and the <u>father</u> <u>of</u> <u>lies</u>" (John 8:44).

"God's kindness is meant to lead you to <u>repentance</u>" (Romans 2:4).

Jesus said about the Holy Spirit, *"And when he comes, he will convict the world concerning sin and righteousness and judgment: concerning sin, because they do not <u>believe</u> in me"* (John 16:8-9).

"[Pray] that I may make it <u>clear</u>, which is how I ought to speak" (Colossians 4:4).

Session 5

And let us not grow weary of doing good, for in due season we will reap, if we <u>do</u> <u>not</u> <u>give</u> <u>up</u>. (Galatians 6:9)

"For the mouth speaks out of that which <u>fills</u> the heart" (Matthew 12:34).

In 2 Timothy 2:24, we learn that the Lord's servant must correct his opponents *"with <u>gentleness</u>. God may perhaps grant them repentance leading to a knowledge of the truth."*

"I have stored up your word in my <u>heart</u>, that I might not sin against you" (Psalm 119:11).

Session 6

"Those who sow in tears shall <u>reap</u> with shouts of joy! He who goes out weeping, bearing the seed for sowing, shall come home with shouts of joy, bringing his sheaves with him" (Psalm 126:5-6).

"Truly, truly, I say to you, unless one is <u>born</u> <u>again</u> he cannot see the kingdom of God" (John 3:3).

Session 7

"But we were <u>gentle</u> among you, like a nursing <u>mother</u> taking care of her own children" (1 Thessalonians 2:7).

"For you know how, like a <u>father</u> with his children, we <u>exhorted</u> each one of you and <u>encouraged</u> you and charged you to walk in a manner worthy of God, who calls you into his own kingdom and glory" (1 Thessalonians 2:11-12).